Cow Power

Kim Riley

Illustrated by
Deb Hinde

RANDOM HOUSE
NEW ZEALAND

It rained, and it rained.
All day and all night it rained.

Cow Number 569 was cold and wet.
The paddock was full of big puddles.
569 was not happy.

Late in the night, the council rang Farmer Riley
to tell her that all the rivers were rising.
She got up to shift her milking cows to higher ground.
Then she went back to bed.

Early next morning, when it was still dark,
569 waited with the other cows for Farmer Riley.
It was time to go in for milking.

Now the water was up to her knees.
'I don't like this one bit,' thought 569.

The cows were all grumbling.
"What has happened to our paddock?" they moaned.

The water was rising fast and soon the gateway was flooded.
"We can't go through there," said the cows.

"Here comes Farmer Riley on her tractor," said 569.
"She'll know what to do."

Farmer Riley climbed off her tractor and looked at the water that filled the gateway.

"We'll have to use the other gateway," she said, "where the water is not so deep."

"No way!" the cows mooed. "We are not going that way, either!" They milled, they turned, then they ran to the back of the paddock. Here the water was even deeper.

"Silly girls," said Farmer Riley. "Wrong way! Turn around!"

"Bail up, bail up!" she shouted, running after the cows.

The cows did not listen — they kept on running.
569 ran too. And then . . .

. . . 569 was floating. So were the other cows.
Farmer Riley was floating, too!

'Mooooo!' thought 569. 'I'm swimming!'
She didn't fight the current —
she just swam along with it, following the cows ahead.

Farmer Riley was also swimming,
but she didn't want to go with the current.
She wanted to get back to safety.
She swam and she swam but the current was too strong.

Farmer Riley tried to grab a tree as she floated by.
But she missed.
Next, Farmer Riley tried to grab a tall post as she floated by.
But she missed.

Then whoosh! . . . Glub, glub, glub!
A cow swam over the top of Farmer Riley
and she swallowed a mouthful of water.
Yuck! It tasted horrible!

She tried to touch the ground,
but her feet got caught up in a barbed-wire fence.
She kicked off her heavy milking boots and on she went,
drifting with the cows on the current.

A little way off, Farmer Riley could see the top of a hill.
There were some cows standing on it.

'I have to swim to that hill before I am washed
into the big river,' thought Farmer Riley.
But she was getting too tired to swim.

Farmer Riley felt something behind her.
A cow, like a big boat, was coming towards her.
It was 569.

'She is going to run me over,' thought Farmer Riley. 'I must get out of her way.'

But, as 569 swam past, Farmer Riley slipped her arm over the cow's neck. She could feel 569's warm, strong body as the cow towed her along.

569 saw the cows safe on the hill
and then she knew what to do.

'Farmer Riley needs my help,' she thought.
She swam for the hill, pulling Farmer Riley to dry land.

Farmer Riley and 569 sat still,
looking at the water all around them.

"Oh, you old darling, 569 — you ugly old thing. You saved me!" cried Farmer Riley, and she patted the cow.

Together they climbed the hill to join the other cows. At last, Farmer Riley and her herd were safe!